"The Only Woman"

"The reality of prejudices and discrimination"

By
Hazeljean Cheeseman Adams

authorHOUSE

1663 LIBERTY DRIVE, SUITE 200
BLOOMINGTON, INDIANA 47403
(800) 839-8640
www.authorhouse.com

This book is a work of non-fiction. Names of people and places have been changed to protect their privacy.

*© 2004 Hazeljean Cheeseman Adams.
All Rights Reserved.*

No part of this book may be reproduced, stored in a retrieval system, or transmitted by any means without the written permission of the author.

First published by AuthorHouse 05/24/04

ISBN: 1-4184-2185-5 (sc)

*Printed in the United States of America
Bloomington, Indiana*

THE ONLY WOMAN

"The reality of prejudices and discrimination"

Author:
Hazeljean Cheeseman Adams

Artist:
David Brokaw

Editor:
Donald Earl Romans

ABOUT THE AUTHOR

The author was the only woman in the majority of her college and career experiences. Out of her "love" and talent for Mathematics and Science she chose a field that seemed reasonable. However being raised in an environment that did not distinguish "boy" and "girl" interest as being different, she was naïve about the "real" world of discrimination that she was facing.

In the 50's she was an anomaly, being the only woman in her mathematics classes. She was pioneer entering the engineering and technical field which was considered a men's field. And also a pioneer in the computer field which was in its early stages in that timeframe.

She was the first woman manager in her company in the mid-1980's and first woman director a few years later. Because of the positions she held she was usually the only women at conferences and management meetings.

Being a female in this male dominated environment, she always felt she was being viewed and evaluated by a different yardstick. Any mistake would be magnified versus a male making the same mistake. Also she had to be very cautious related to her emotions to avoid be labeled an "emotional" female.

On the positive side, being involved in a leading-edge technical field she had the opportunity to work on very interesting projects. She worked on some of the computer applications for the early space program, as well as software for many other defense related applications.

Also she was on the Internet before Al Gore "invented it". It was actually the ARPANET, a government network that was a precursor to the Internet.

She has had a home computer since 1979. She owned one of the first Commodore Pet Personal Computers. In her "retirement" she continues to keep up with the latest computer technology. She volunteers doing Web pages for the local library, teaches and helps new computer users in her church and the community in general. Also she continues to do programming and consulting projects.

PREFACE

This book is comprised of a series of stories describing situations resulting from being the Only Woman "caught" in a male-dominated world. The author has attempted to keep the book on the "light" side, since many of stories are funny in retrospect. These incidents were actually very hurtful and some were even degrading at the time they occurred. Other stories are not intended to be amusing. They describe the realities of discrimination and "double-standards" facing a female trying to compete (or even survive) in a male dominated technical field. The impact of the incidents described in the book may be difficult for someone to fully understand who has not walked in the shoes of a minority.

TABLE OF CONTENTS

GET YOUR HANDS OFF OF ME 1

NOW IS THE HOUR 4

TONY WHO? 8

MOVE OVER GUYS... HERE I COME 12

MARRIED WOMAN ONLY? 18

UP, UP, AND AWAY 22

TRIP TO CHICAGO 26

A SLIGHT ADJUSTMENT 28

SORRY, SOME "NERD" TALK 30

CHEMICAL PLANT SIMULATION PROJECT 33

RESEARCH LAB 36

SOMETIMES THE ONLY WAY UP IS OUT 38

ENCOUNTER WITH LOCAL UNION EXECUTIVES .. 43

TEACHING ASSIGNMENT AT A MILITARY BASE 53

A PERIOD OF UNCERTAINTY 55

A NEW ERA IN COMPUTING 58

FIRST WOMAN MANAGER 62

IS SHE IN HERE? 67

MANAGEMENT PHYSICAL EXAMINATIONS 70

THE COMPUTER CLUB 72

HOME COMPUTERS	75
"GET HER OUT OF MY OFFICE"	77
RADIO INTERVIEW	80
FIRST WOMAN DIRECTOR	82
CONFERENCES	85
HOW I SURVIVED AGAINST MANY ODDS	87
SPECIAL PROJECTS	89
HARASSMENT	92
DEALING WITH THE UNION	95
PRESSURE FROM VP	97
BOSS'S NIGHT	101
DOUBLE STANDARD ISSUE: FRIENDS WITH SUBORDINATES	104
DOUBLE STANDARD: EMOTIONS	106
"RETIREMENT"	108

FORWARD

This book is intended to describe the trials and tribulations of a young woman entering a so-called "man's field" in the mid 1950's.

I was the only woman in my college math and engineering classes, the only woman working in a small company, the only woman manager, and finally, the only woman director.

There were many tough and discouraging times. I have often wondered if it was worth it. It would have been much easier to have settled for a "traditional" field for woman. But if I had chosen a traditional career, I would not be writing this book.

I have tried to keep the book on the "light side". In retrospect many of my experiences are funny now. But when they occurred they were not very amusing. Even though there is less discrimination today than in the 1950's, things have not really changed that much. Laws have changed…but attitudes are slow to change.

In those times the discrimination was blatant. Today it is not so obvious, but it still exists. I had a female friend recently leave a local company because of a form of discrimination. She has a PHD in engineering. She left to take a teaching position at a University. Her supervisor and co-workers (all male) would not listen to her ideas and basically ignored her. This too is a form of discrimination. However, it is very difficult to prove.

In addition to discrimination in the workplace, I faced discrimination in other areas. In my early thirties, I tried to buy income property. I was a single female. I believe I was discriminated against on both counts. Another member of my family (male) got a loan from the same bank in the same timeframe for a similar amount. At that time our salaries were comparable.

A male co-worker offered to make an offer for the same house and apply at the same bank so I would have a valid claim for a suit. I should have taken legal action, but decided it wasn't worth the hassle and stress involved.

The seeds of discrimination are planted at a very early age. I still hear young parents today say to their small children: "Little girls don't do this or that". I recently volunteered in a local grade school and heard the teachers making similar statements. Young minds are easy to mold and teachers have a huge influence on them.

BABY CHEESEMAN

GET YOUR HANDS OFF OF ME

I was born in a medium size town, the second of three children. My family would be considered in the low middle class category. My Dad always had a job, though not a high paying job, but adequate for our lifestyle. My parents were very generous people and we had an "open door" policy for all relatives that needed help. So we almost always had someone in addition to the immediate family living with us. If anyone in the family did not have a job they would just move in.

We lived in an older downtown neighborhood and did not own a car until I was six years old. My Dad walked to work since it was less than a half mile. My Mother walked to shop for groceries, clothes, etc. And all the kids all walked to school. We used the car only to visit relatives in a suburb of Cleveland or for summer vacations.

My parents did not have a formal education. Both of my parents were raised on a farm. My Mother went to school only part of the year. She was taken out of school to work on the farm during planting and harvest seasons. My Dad left school at an early age to go to work. Both of my parents were very intelligent and accomplished much even with limited formal education.

My parents believed that if someone received a good education the sky was the limit regarding what they could achieve. I was encouraged at a very early age to get a good education.

I always wanted to go to college from the time I was about 4 years old. I remember going to visit a cousin when I was very small. He was going to graduate school and had a den in the basement where he studied. I can remember going there and being intrigued by all his books. I decided right then that I was going to college. At that age I had no concept of what really was involved in going to college. I had no idea what career I would choose. I am sure I didn't even know what "career" meant. I was just fascinated by all the books and associated the books with college.

I have always been a strong-willed person. From the very beginning I was very independent. Because of my independent attitude, my Dad once said. "I bet when the doctor smacked you on the butt when you were born, you told him to get his hands off of you". I truly believe that this independence and strong will is the reason I survived all the barriers and hassles in my career.

NOW IS THE HOUR

Even though college was my goal I started out hating school. I did not want to go at all. I gave my Mother a difficult time for the first three grades. In fact, I had to be forced to go to school every day. But after that early rebellion, I began to love school. I always loved mathematics and science. I always felt that if I worked hard I could do anything anyone else could do. Because of my parent's attitude toward education and lack of any prejudices, I grew up totally naïve regarding discrimination because of gender

My independent nature gave me the strength to battle all odds, even during my early years. I would in those days be considered a "tom-boy" I liked all sports, and played football. baseball, basketball etc with the neighborhood boys. My parents always let me do what I wanted to do if it was not immoral or illegal. They never once said to me "you should not do that because you are a girl" I had toy cars and electric trains at a very young age. I also had dolls, but never played with them. I just loved to collect them and kept them for many years. I also loved stuffed animals, and still do. I currently have a collection of several hundred TY Beanie Babies

My interest in science and mathematics made me "different", even in grade school. But I did not mind being different. I was encouraged by most of my teachers. Most girls did not share my interests. So at an early age I was kind of the "ONLY" girl.

I had many interests beside mathematics, science, and sports. I liked music and took piano and clarinet lessons for several years. However, I was not very talented when it came to manual skills, thus I never became very skilled in the music areas.

In the eighth grade I had a male teacher for the first time. He was a retired army officer. He was one of my better teachers. Like my parents he made no distinction between "boy" and "girl" things. He treated the girls as equals with the boys. This was very rare at that time. We had a mixed male and female baseball team. He even taught all of us military maneuvers.

Today all this would be considered good physical fitness. But at that time, this teacher was criticized for allowing girls and boys to join in these activities. Thank goodness he was a maverick and did not cave in to the pressure.

If you are wondering about the title of this section, a popular song of my eighth grade graduation was "Now Is the Hour". For the graduation I wrote the following lyrics to go with the tune: "Now Is the Hour"

"Now is the hour
When we must say Good-Bye

"The Only Woman"

Eight years of study.

Oh how the time did fly.

Soon we will be leaving.

Friends and teachers too.

But we will remember.

The times we spent with you."

TONY WHO?

In high school I was able to concentrate on my mathematics and took all the math courses that were offered at the time. In addition, I became very interested in writing. As a sophomore I was "invited" (forced by my English instructor) to start writing for the school newspaper. As I look back on that experience I am very grateful to that teacher. Up to that point I had been the typical "nerd" mathematical type. I was also quite introverted. Writing for the school newspaper expanded my horizon significantly.

I became the Editor of the school newspaper as a junior and in my senior year became editor of the year book. In this endeavor I learned leadership and management skills that I used later in my career. In those positions I had to "manage" my peers (a bunch of rowdy teenagers) to meet deadlines and get the paper out on schedule without errors. With all the other activities these students were involved in, this was NOT an easy task. In that time it was unusual for a "girl" to have a major "leadership" role, even in the journalism area.

I received several awards for writing during high school. As a result, when I graduated I was offered a writing job at the local newspaper. Since I was determined to go to college and major in mathematics, I turned down that position.

In my senior year I tested for several scholarships and was able to get a scholarship at a local university for my first year of college. I graduated from high school as Valedictorian of my class with my highest grades being in mathematics and science. I also was selected by my peers to receive the Womanhood cup award. This was an award for the outstanding woman in all areas….citizenship, leadership, as well as scholastic achievement. These early achievements gave me a great feeling of satisfaction and encouragement.

While in high school Tony Bennett visited our school.

Actually he was virtually unknown at the time so it was no big deal. I remember escorting him since I was a hall guard at the time of the visit. He visited our school along with a local disc jockey, Jack Clifton. Sad to say, Jack Clifton died shortly after this visit with stomach cancer. No one else seems to remember this visit. I have tried to verify the visit with the local radio station where Jack Clifton worked. But they cannot verify that Tony Bennett visited our school, but did verify that he visited our town in that timeframe.

"The Only Woman"

COLLEGE MATH CLASS

MOVE OVER GUYS...
HERE I COME

The title of this book "The ONLY Woman" took on meaning even in my college days. I was the ONLY woman in the family to attend and graduate from college. My Dad and Mother never dreamed that after getting a college education, I would have difficulty getting a job in my chosen field. My Dad passed away when I was a senior in college and did not experience the difficulties that I encountered after graduation. My Mother lived several years after that and shared in the difficulties and disappointments in my career.

When I entered the university on a scholarship, I knew I wanted to do something in mathematics or science area.

"The Only Woman"

But I was discouraged by my advisors and decided to major in accounting. In the accounting area I was also the ONLY woman in most of my classes. After a year and half in accounting, I was totally bored and consequently changed my major to Mathematics, to what I wanted from the beginning. Again I was discouraged by my advisors.

I was the ONLY woman in all of my Mathematics classes. Most the Mathematics classes at that time were composed of male engineering students. Even though there was one other woman engineering student she was a few years ahead of me and not in any of my classes.

Being the ONLY woman I tried twice as hard to prove myself. And I found myself competing with two of the top male engineering students to get the best grades in the classes. I didn't always surpass them. We alternated getting the best grades. And I was always disappointed if I received a lower grade than them. I also took several Engineering courses as electives and competed with the same guys there, also.

Hazeljean Cheeseman Adams

I had two female mathematics instructors. Females were accepted as teachers of mathematics, but they would not have been accepted in industry. I am sure that is the reason they chose the teaching field, but I doubt that they received equal pay with the male professors.

Since I had no idea what career possibilities were available to mathematics majors, I also decided to take education courses, so that I would be qualified to teach mathematics, in case I needed an alternative career path.

Being the ONLY woman always made it more difficult. If I skipped class it was very obvious. If one of the guys missed, no one would notice.

Also, I always felt I was being "picked on" by the instructors. One female instructor in particular ALWAYS called on me to solve a problem in front of the class. I was never sure if she was picking on me because I was the ONLY woman or maybe to show the guys what I could do.

"The Only Woman"

Or maybe it was because my name was the only name she could remember. Regardless of the reason, I had to always be prepared. As a result I had to work harder. In retrospect this was actually very beneficial to me. All these experiences made me more resilient to all the battles that I would face in the future.

The one male professor that I had was much more supportive of me than the female professors. I never quite understood that. Maybe they perceived my future challenges and wanted to make me more resilient.

This male professor was tough on everyone and treated me equal with the guys, which of course, is the way I wanted to be treated.

Since my Dad had a stroke and became disabled when I was a freshman in college, finishing college was a financial struggle. I received a scholarship for my senior year that was given to the outstanding senior woman at my university. Even though I worked during my college years, the scholarships made finishing in four years possible.

I worked at a local department store in the credit department. I was kind of a "jack of all trades" and did a lot of jobs that no one else wanted to do. But this variety was also beneficial to me toward my future career. My boss was considered a tyrant and was disliked by everyone. However he was very supportive of me. His son was in line for his position and he was close to retirement. When I was in my senior year at the university he offered me his son's position when he retired and his son moved up. I did not turn it down formally. But this was not a position that interested me.

The position was Credit Manager. I wanted a position in the technical field utilizing my educational background. When I was close to graduation the boss called me into his office one day and said "with your talent you would be a fool to stay here, go out there and get a position in you area of expertise". Of course I took this advice because I wasn't really interested in staying there anyway.

"The Only Woman"

HIRING MARRIED WOMAN ONLY?

MARRIED WOMAN ONLY?

I graduated from college with two majors, Mathematics and Secondary Education. I was qualified to teach in three fields: Mathematics, Business, and French. I had considered teaching but after my one semester observing in a local junior high school, I decided teaching was not for me.

So after graduation I began looking for a job with the local tire companies. I wanted to stay in my home town and all the large companies were tire companies.

At the first company, I was interviewed by people in the Human Resources area. They were all impressed by my educational background, my grades, and my references.

"The Only Woman"

The human resources person called the supervisor who had the opening for a Math Major. As they described my qualifications he was very interested and ready to hire me. The human resources interviewer said "great we will send her to your office". Until he heard the word HER the supervisor assumed I was a male candidate. When he realized I was female. His comment was: "this job requires the person to work in the factory. We can't have a woman working in the factory….especially an unmarried woman". The interviewer was very apologetic but said that he could do nothing for me. And that was the end of the interview.

At another company, the interviews went well until I was asked if I could type by the final interviewer. I thought I was being interviewed for a technical position. But the position was a clerk position and the person had to run an adding machine and type. I could have qualified for this job after high school. I certainly did not need a degree in Mathematics. They said they had no other positions for "a woman".

I had a few other disappointing interviews with smaller companies with similar results. I was very discouraged and was about to give up and go back to the teaching alternative.

A male friend that I graduated with had been hired by a subsidiary of one of the rubber companies. He had the same degree as I received. He recommended that I try interviewing there, which I did. I was hired by the company but in a position way below my educational background. After four years of college and Bachelors degree in Mathematics, this position paid a lower salary than I was offered at the newspaper when I graduated from high school.

This was one of my first lessons regarding selecting a "non-traditional" field for woman. I was very disillusioned at the time. And I felt I had wasted four years of my life. I accepted the position even though it was below my educational level. But it was a job. And I needed to make a living.

"The Only Woman"

My job classification was Computist. I think they made it up just for me. I was the only one with that classification for several years. The initial job function was to operate an X/Y plotting machine. Four years of college Mathematics to watch a little machine produce X-Y graphs. I could have performed this job after the eighth grade. I was totally bored with this repetitive routine job.

Then one day I met my college friend who had recommended the company to me. He had the same degree as me and had been hired as a Development Engineer at almost twice the salary that I was receiving. I still get sick to my stomach when I think about this. It was very disappointing but I needed to work and had no other options.

UP, UP, AND AWAY

The company had a computer department. However, this was during the very early stages of computer technology. The company was considered a high technology company with the majority of its contracts being with the Defense Department. With my mathematics degree, I thought my best opportunities would be in the computer programming area.

I kept asking my immediate supervisor for the opportunity to learn to program. Finally one day he gave me a computer manual and told me that he would allow me some time each day to get on the computer and teach myself to program. I spent a couple hours each day "teaching" myself to program in machine language. The computer manuals then, like now, were very cryptic and difficult to understand. After several months, I was able to program, after a fashion. Shortly after this the company upgraded the computer. It was fortunate that I had pressed the issue and was programming when this upgrade occurred. The computer company, IBM provided formal programmer training classes for the new computer.

So I finally had an opportunity to progress faster with the formal training, rather than the slow process of trying to teach myself from the manual.

One of my early assignments was to develop software for the "lighter than air" vehicles. I helped develop programs for the Blimp's first electronically controlled light signs. The program actually caused the lights to show movement of cartoon characters and of course the company name and advertising slogans. This was a very tedious program at that time and was done in machine language. However, it was a fun job and I was happy for the opportunity. Another "lighter than air" project was the V-balloon project. We developed a lighter than air vehicle to be used to transport large logs over rough terrain. I am not sure this application was ever fully implemented, but it was an intriguing and challenging project. The V-balloon was actually used as a "skyhook" to support the logs and rigging used to transport the logs.

The recent Columbia spacecraft disaster brings to mind another early programming assignment. I worked on a program that simulated various space vehicle re-entry speeds and the effect of the resulting temperatures on the protective heat-shield tiles. The program simulated the effect of very high temperatures on various materials and tile thickness. This process is called ablation. The high temperatures caused the tiles to ablate (flake) away thus protecting the spacecrafts aluminum alloy frame from burning, and breaking up off the spacecraft. Of course, over the years, materials, thickness etc I am sure have changed significantly. But I am sure programs are still being written to simulate the changing environmental conditions experienced by space vehicles.

"The Only Woman"

I also worked on the early trajectory analysis programs that simulated various orbits, speeds and atmospheric conditions that affected the early manned and unmanned space travel missions.

TRIP TO CHICAGO

My first trip for the company was to Chicago for an IBM class. I went with two men…my boss and a co-worker. The youngest was fifteen years my senior. I was about twenty four at the time.

Traveling with a female co-worker was a new experience for the guys. We usually went to eat together in the evening. I am sure I inhibited their usually activities while traveling. One day, I overheard them talking outside my hotel room. The discussion was about their desire to visit a burlesque show but they had a dilemma. They did not know what to do with me. They did not want to leave me alone. And they were not sure about asking me to join them. But they decided they would casually mention it to me to see how I reacted. They did not know I had overheard their conversation.

But I was ready. As soon as they mentioned going to the burlesque show I said:" No problem. I will go with you". But it was the most ridiculous evening I ever spent in my life. I don't remember if I was the ONLY woman in the audience. But odds are that I was the ONLY woman.

For years, I did not share this story with anyone, but my Mother. Actually I was too embarrassed to discuss it with anyone, and at that time those guys were not about to mention it to anyone either.

A SLIGHT ADJUSTMENT

After getting the formal computer training at IBM, I finally started to have more opportunities to program. However there was no change in classification or salary but at least I had a chance for a less boring job. And that was the beginning of my computer "career". I went back to school at night and took additional computer and engineering courses and finally got myself off the plotting machine and into a full time programming position.

My classification was finally changed to Development Engineer about 4 years after graduating. This was the title that the men received when they hired-in directly after graduating. Since this was early in the computer era, there

"The Only Woman"

were no specific titles for computer people. Anyone with a technical degree was given the title of Development Engineer.

After working for two or three more years in the computer department, I was given more responsibility. I was really performing a group leader function without the title. I actually had younger, less experienced men reporting to me that had higher salaries than me. I had also trained them. This inequity in salary and titles continued for far too many years.

After a few more years I became the ONLY female section head in the engineering organization. I still had men reporting to me that had higher salaries.

However, at this point many of the men were much older and had more service and it was somewhat reasonable for them to have higher salaries.

SORRY, SOME "NERD" TALK

Most of my early programming experience was in machine or assembler language. Later on in my career I was very thankful that I had started my career in the era of machine language programming. This experience gave me more depth and a better understanding of the hardware. This was invaluable knowledge to prepare me for future job opportunities in the company.

In the early nineteen sixties the first high level programming language was introduced. It was called Fortransit….later became FORTRAN. I became very fluent in the FORTRAN language. The company started a training program to teach engineers this programming language.

"The Only Woman"

Most of the engineers graduated prior to the introduction of the computer and had no formal computer training. They had no computer programming classes at the university level.

Since I had taken more computer training at the university and had knowledge of FORTRAN I became the instructor. I enjoyed teaching and programming…the perfect combination. I developed training material to supplement the inadequate computer manuals provided by the computer manufacturer. Actually this was a neat little niche for me. Also teaching by a female was well accepted, and besides, none of the guys really wanted to do it. I continued to teach, develop new software, and perform as a Section Head.

As Section Head I was in charge of Operating System Software and Computer Operations. In this position I was responsible for the operation of all the engineering computer equipment and supporting personnel. This was a position which required 24 hour support. As a result I was often called in the middle of the night it the computer went down for any reason.

OOPS!

WARDROBE CHANGE REQUIRED

CHEMICAL PLANT SIMULATION PROJECT

I was assigned to do an Operation Research project for a chemical processing plant. I had to develop equations and then work in the plant to collect data for the simulation. When I went to the plant I discovered that all the floors were grated. I was wearing high heels at the time and my high heels went through the grated floors. There had never been woman in the plant before. So I had to change my shoes in order to walk in the plant.

It was a huge simulation project. I worked on the project with a male co-worker. When the project was completed the model consisted of about two hundred equations with two hundred variables. The company's computer was not big enough to handle a problem of that size and we had to travel to a government facility to use their computer to complete the project. It was another great learning experience.

"The Only Woman"

HMMMM? NO LADIES RESTROOM

RESEARCH LAB

I was assigned to do a simulation project at a research laboratory at a university. After arriving at the facility I discovered that the building where I was working did not have a woman's restroom. They had not had a woman at that building and I guess were not planning on any in the future. I was shocked and upset at the time. To use the restroom, I had to go to an adjoining building where there was a female receptionist. I could not believe it. But in hind site, it makes an amusing story.

This was a simulation project related to long term space travel. My assignment was the simulation of the growth of plants to provide food for space travelers. It involved

"The Only Woman"

developing a math model and computer program to simulate the growth of various plants. This project was actually a team project shared with a university.

SOMETIMES THE ONLY WAY UP IS OUT

After twelve years at the company, I felt I was in a dead-end "service oriented" position. My boss was only a couple years older than me. And he was not moving up because there were no growth opportunities in our division. It was very difficult to move within the company.

There were a couple of opportunities for me to move in the company, but I was not permitted to move. In this company if your supervisor did not approve a lateral transfer, you could not move. Even though these were lateral moves, I felt there was more opportunity for advancement sooner in other areas.

"The Only Woman"

So, I decided to leave the company. In a large company (male or female) you can get trapped in a dead-end position, and that is where I found myself. Being female and knowing that the prejudices were still out there, I was a little apprehensive about starting at the bottom again in another large company. I am not sure I would have even been hired in the larger companies because of my gender. The candidate companies were the same companies I had approached earlier with no success.

So I joined a small high-tech company. I was the seventeenth employee to join the company, and yes the ONLY woman holding a technical position. We were all prior employees of my previous employer. There was one other female in a clerical position

With the small company, I had several more ONLY woman experiences. I did marketing as well as technical work for the company. I did internal programming for the company's business requirements such as payroll, accounts payable and accounts receivable. This was my first experience programming in a non-technical application. My college accounting course became an asset in these areas. I also did contract programming for outside customers. Typical customers were civil engineers, architects, and a local labor union, etc. These companies were too small to support a full time programmer and therefore contracted for programming as required. I was not just the ONLY technical woman in my company; I was also the ONLY woman at the customer sites.

This situation led to some new and different problems. I guess in the larger company I was somewhat sheltered from the real world. In the small company I found myself being propositioned by customers.

Also we almost lost a large contract because the 'decision maker' wanted me to be included as a part of the contract. This person called me daily, sent me cards and letters, etc which would be considered stalking today. The contract which he was awarding was a significant contact for our

"The Only Woman"

company. Losing it could cause a disaster for a company our size.

I endured this harassment for several months. I never had face to face contact with this man unless one of my co-workers was present. After this went on for awhile one of my co-workers advised me to take some action against this man and described him as being "sick". My co-worker's comment to me was "if we lose the contact, so be it".

I decided to wait a few days until the deadline for the decision. I avoided the guy and ignored his calls and letters.

We did finally win the contract. After the fact, we believe he really was not the one who made the final decision. He was telling us that he had the final decision in order to get some perks. The day we received the written contact I called this louse on the phone with three witnesses in the room. What I said to him cannot be published. Thank goodness my male co-workers were willing to lose this contract to support me. In today's world I could have sued. But in the early 1970's suing was not an option.

In this small company we could not afford the overhead of our own computer. Instead we leased computer time from other area companies that had excess capacity. I developed software and then went to various sites to use whatever computer best suited the application.

Most of the applications were in the structural analysis area. However I did a variety of applications, including payroll, statistical analysis, etc. Since I was the only technical software person in the company I did internal programs to support the design engineers. Again this was a good opportunity to learn about computer hardware design.

ENCOUNTER WITH LOCAL UNION EXECUTIVES

While at the small computer company I had a programming project to do statistical analysis for a local labor union. Of course in this environment I was the only woman. In presenting the proposal I sat alone across the long table with about a dozen male union executives on the other side. They were a bunch of paunchy old guys with cigars. They resembled the Mafia characters in the movies.

Talk about intimidation. As I was giving the presentation I realized from the questions they were asking that they had no idea what I was talking about. I could have been speaking in French. In the middle I abandoned my formal presentation and started talking to them in their language. It worked and I got the job. It was about a one-year project. I am not sure if they ever used the results. The young man from the union that I worked with was about my age. He was making twice what I was making, plus he had a lot of perks such as car, free meals etc. Of course, this inequality was very upsetting to me.

As often happens in small companies there was a slump in the economy and the small company had financial difficulties. I bailed out just before my position was about to be eliminated.

Since there were no opportunities in the area for technical software people, I decided to look for a position in the business application area.

I was able to find a business programming position in a medium sized company. My university accounting and business classes became an asset in acquiring this position. I took this as a temporary position to gain more knowledge in the business application area. I did not consider it as a permanent or long term situation.

The company promised to move me to a technical position in manufacturing when there was an opening. I did have the opportunity to work in the plant occasionally.

But it was a union shop and the union members objected to having their work monitored by online computers. Several times the computer cables were "intentionally" cut by someone in the plant. I quickly became very bored in this position and felt waiting for the full time technical position would be longer than I would be able to tolerate. So again I decided to search for a teaching position in the computer science field at area universities.

MY FAVORITE BOSS AND MENTOR

A NEW BEGINNING AT AGE 37

The day before I had planned to accept a teaching position at a local university, I received a call from a manager at my previous employer with an offer to rejoin the company in a new position in an exciting new business area.

The company was developing a new computer called a parallel processor and needed programmers to develop operating system software for the new computer. A very exciting "ground floor" opportunity, I thought. Even though I had sworn never to return to the company, the challenge of the project was something I could not pass up.

Also this specific manager influenced my decision. He was very enthusiastic about the project and "sold" me on the future of the project and my future in the company. What is interesting about this, is that if I had remained at the company I would probably not been allowed to move to this position from within the company.

Yes, I was the ONLY woman in the initial group. However a few women joined the team in later years. When I returned to my previous employer, I stated that I preferred to stay in a technical and not be in management again. But my new boss encouraged me and insisted that I consider a management position again. He felt that I had management skills and I would be wasted in a technical position. And with in a year I was a group leader and within three years I was a Section head again.

This Manager was the best boss I had in my entire career. He had absolutely no prejudices. He judged everyone on the basis of their talent and performance. He is probably responsible for my future advances in the company. He treated me like "one of the guys". He treated everyone who worked for him with respect. Also if you did a good job he told you immediately. He did not wait for the "annual" review. I was called to his office many times just to get a "pat on the back" for something I had done. This was so unusual in this company that the first time I was called to his office I though I was going to be fired.

Because of this boss's treatment of the people who reported to everyone went beyond the call of duty… including me. It was very unfortunate that he was diagnosed with cancer of the lung at the age of 47 and only lived about 18 months. Loosing him was a large let down for the project, the people on the project, and especially me.

I will never forget the last day he was able to work; he came to my desk and gave me a final boost. He said "you are very talented and will go far…just keep up the good work". He also said "this project will be successful, you will be here to see it, but I won't".

Unfortunately, the project never reached its potential after his death. Partly because his enthusiasm in the project was unique and could not be replaced. The man who replaced him had a difficult job "filling his shoes", especially with the people on the project. In fact this manager said to me in the heat of an argument one day. "You people would not be happy if Jesus Christ himself replaced Jack."

There was a "glass ceiling" for woman at the Section Head position. There had never been a female department manager. If my boss had not died at age 49, I am sure that glass ceiling would have been broken sooner. So I continued as section head for several years.

In this position I was responsible for system software development. I also became a Project Manager for one of the remote customer installation sites. I was in charge of the in-.house training facility. Potential customers did not have the computer at their site. They came to our in-house training facility to learn to program the computer prior to their computer being installed.

In addition to teaching at our site, I traveled to future customer sites to teach programming. All of these sites were within the Department of Defense.

In addition to training I was in charge of a team that developed the manuals and training materials for the computer. I was also involved in writing proposals for potential customers.

I personally wrote the Programmer's user manual for the new computer. Performing this task became quite a challenge. There was only one person in the world who totally understood his computer…the inventor. He was an extremely intelligent person, but not the world's best communicator. The computer was very complex and since it was a parallel processor, it was nothing like the conventional computer of that timeframe. In order to write the manual I had to understand totally how each instruction worked.

"The Only Woman"

Sometimes in order to understand the instruction I had to go to the inventor, describe what I thought the instruction did…in English, and ask him for a "yes" or "no" answer. As a result of this I became very knowledgeable about every aspect of the computer.

Therefore I became the primary software instructor. I traveled and taught with the inventor. He taught the hardware architecture and I taught the software development portion.

Again I find myself in the teaching arena. Is that because it is considered a "woman's field"? I am not sure, but I was reasonably happy in this role.

Hazeljean Cheeseman Adams

ONLY WOMAN IN MOTEL

TEACHING ASSIGNMENT AT A MILITARY BASE

I was teaching at a Military base with a co-worker...male of course. All of the students were men. Some of them were in the military. Some were professors at a local university. They were being trained to program a computer that my company had developed. I was the ONLY woman in the motel where all the students were staying. I had an adjoining room to two of the male students. The adjoining door did not look too secure. Out of fear I moved furniture against the door.

The following story is interesting but has nothing to do with me being a woman. The two students in the adjoining room were professors from the University. Every night they discussed very loudly what was presented in the class during the day. They had no idea the Instructor was in the adjoining room….thank goodness. Every night I listened to all their criticisms. They were not criticizing the instructors however. They were critiquing the computer's "deficiencies". Since I had heard their comments, the next day I would go to class prepared to counteract their criticisms.

Most of the criticisms were not valid, but only because they had a miss-understanding of the computers capabilities. So each day I would respond to the criticism with a clarification of the computer's capabilities. Only my boss and I knew this story until recent years. I now feel free to share it.

A PERIOD OF UNCERTAINTY

After my boss's premature death from cancer, the enthusiasm for the new computer diminished at all levels. He was the super promoter of this technology. I again found myself looking around the company for a new position. I had an offer to go to the parent company to manage the computer facility. It was a great opportunity for me, but I was not allowed to transfer.

During this time period I was loaned out to other areas that needed software help. I was on assignment for several months in the Flight Simulator area. I also went one day a week to another company location to support the computer system that monitored the centrifuges on a nuclear enrichment project.

I was often "loaned out" to work on the computer software portions on proposals in other areas of the company, when they needed someone with computer software expertise. I was also on selection committees when the company was acquiring special purpose computers, such as Automated drafting systems, Computer Aided Design and Computer Aided Manufacturing systems, Automated Publication Systems, Personal Computers, etc. Proposal writing was very mundane to me, but the opportunity to be on the selection committee was very interesting and challenging. It also broadened my knowledge in other areas of the company.

In this role I helped develop specifications for the systems. I traveled to potential supplier sites to evaluate the proposed systems. When the systems were acquired I helped train our company personal to operate and manage these

"The Only Woman"

systems. I continued these assignments even after I became a Manager.

In the early 1980s the Department Manager of the Engineering Computer Services was promoted to a corporate position. With my broad background in the computer field, I was a candidate to replace him.

A NEW ERA IN COMPUTING
MY MOTTO "A TERMINAL ON EVERY DESK"

My career as a female in the computer field was always a struggle just trying to survive. But I had the opportunity to see the evolution of computers which was exciting and kept the job challenging and interesting.

When I began my career in the late fifties the computer filled several rooms and cost several million dollars. Now the lap top that I am using to write this book is much more powerful and cost less than $1500. Also the early machines used punched cards and punched paper tape as input. Actually the punched cards and tape continued into the eighties until timesharing and remote terminals were introduced.

"The Only Woman"

In the early days programmers developed the programs on paper. Then the programs were punched into cards by keypunchers on punched card machines. With the advent of remote terminal and timesharing, a programmer could sit at his/her desk and enter the programs directly into the computer. Of course this was much more efficient and programs could be developed in a shorter time-period. But it significantly changed job functions. The keypunching jobs were gradually eliminated. And of course programmers and engineers had to learn how to type, after a fashion. They now had to enter their own programs and data.

This was a difficult transition for some of the older Engineers and a total shock to the traditional engineer managers. So now my job was just not fighting the gender battle but also convincing the "old school managers" that engineers needed terminals on their desks so they could do their jobs working directly interfacing with the computer. Many managers felt that the Engineers were wasting their time working at terminals.

Several of these managers were my age but they had not kept up to date with the rapidly changing computer technology.

However the improvements in efficiency and turn around time for arriving at a solution were much improved. Of course I was a computer person and it was easy for me to see the benefits. But many of the Engineer managers had no concept of how computers functioned. So part of my job in the early 1980's was selling other managers that their employees needed terminals on their desks.

By the mid 80s it was clear the terminals were being replaced with Personal Computers (PCs). At this point many of the problems could be solved locally on the PCs and the PCs also served as terminals to the mainframe computers when the function required more power. Of course it wasn't long until we all realized that the PCs were becoming more powerful and more efficient and cost effective than the large mainframe computers.

"The Only Woman"

GLASS CEILING OR GLASS FLOOR?

FIRST WOMAN MANAGER
GLASS CEILING OR GLASS FLOOR?

When the Manager of Engineering Computer Services position became available, I was well qualified for the position. In fact I had been a Section Head in that Department 10 years earlier prior to leaving the company. I knew the position well. In fact I had often taken the manager's place when he was absent.

Also I had significantly broadened my experience in the meantime. I had gained more technical, business, and management skills. But there were several male competitors for the position. Most of them were much younger than me and none had the diverse experience in the technical

"The Only Woman"

computer field that I had. But they were male and that made the rules different. And there had never been a female at this level.

I heard of all the underground gossip about not wanting a "female in the position" with lots of "flimsy" excuses. Like I would have "Older men reporting to me, some with higher degrees" (the male candidates also had this issue); "could a female handle the stress of this position?" etc.

I felt that I was the best qualified person for the position and had made up my mind that if I did not get it I would leave the company again. After much anxiety on my part, and several weeks of rumors, I did get the position. I would love to know the conversations behind the scenes during that decision making period. I will never know.

But I was challenged at every level. I accepted the challenges and survived in that position regardless of the odds. I felt like I was always being tested and under a microscope. I sometimes felt that instead of a "glass ceiling"

I was walking on a "glass floor". And I felt if I made the slightest mistake, I thought I might go crashing through it. I knew if I made a mistake as a manger it would be magnified because I was a woman.

In my new management position the Computer Department was in a growth mode. More of the typical manual processes were being computerized. I was a strong promoter for getting everything automated.

I was also an advocate for training everyone in the basic computer skills. I developed and taught computer classes to everyone who was willing to attend. Since the company did not have funds for these classes I taught after business hours on my own time with no pay. Also all the students attended with no pay. I taught secretaries, production workers, even managers. Anyone who was willing to attend on their own time was welcome.

Even this mode of training was a result of discrimination. The company had funds to train the engineers but not for

"The Only Woman"

other employees. I had taught FORTRAN programming to Engineers for many years. It was always supported and funded by the company.

Also at this time technology had developed to the point where it was possible to timeshare a computer (many users could be on-line and use the same computer simultaneously). Portable computer terminals became available so employees could use the computer via these terminals anyplace where there was a phone.

I encouraged management to permit employees to borrow these terminals and use them from home. This complemented my training program. An employee could take a computer home to do homework and practice. The employee was benefiting. But the company was also benefiting. The company was essentially getting employees trained FREE. But it was a significant uphill battle to convince the older management to agree to let people take terminals home. It was finally approved and became a very positive program for the company as well as the employees.

It was also a significant selling job to convince management that employees needed terminals and later personal computers at their desks. I spent a lot of time demonstrating to other managers the benefit of distributing of computer equipment throughout the company.

Again I found myself in a training mode, training managers to use computers to automate some of their own routine, repetitive functions, such as employee evaluations, budget management, and salary administration.

As a result of all my efforts beyond "the call of duty", I was awarded the company's Spirit Award in 1980. Also I was the ONLY woman in my division to receive this award.

IS SHE IN HERE?

Having the first female manager in the company also had an affect on the other woman. Most women were very supportive but it did have an effect on their modus operendi.

The ladies restroom was always a favorite place for the woman to talk about their bosses. When I became the first female manager, I inhibited this very healthy outlet. Before the ladies started a conversation they would look at the feet under the stalls to see if I was in there. One day I was in one of the stalls when I heard a conversation in the outer room. One of the ladies said, "Is she in here?" She was very shocked when I responded: "Yes I am in here, but I will be leaving in a few minutes so you can continue your conversation."

"The Only Woman"

MANAGER'S PHYSICAL EXAM DAY

MANAGEMENT PHYSICAL EXAMINATIONS

At my company everyone in a Management position had to have an annual physical examination by the company physician. When I became the first female manager I had to have the physical.

Knowing my boss, I am sure it was intentional that he did not tell the physician that I was female. Everyone went by initials, so they could not detect by the name if the manager was male or female.

The day I appeared for the exam the nurses and doctor were in shock. They had never had a woman before and were not prepared. To prepare for examination I had to remove all my clothes. Since they had never given a physical examination to a woman, they did not have a gown. The nurses were so flustered. They finally found a sheet from one of the examining tables and gave it to me.

The following year when I went for the physical, I took my own hospital gown.

THE COMPUTER CLUB

Another effort to encourage employees to learn the new technology was the establishment of a company computer club. The club was open to employees and their families. At that point another employee and I started training classes for the computer club. This included employee's children. We had several kids "on-line" using computers in the early 1980's. Every time you go out on a limb to encourage new ideas there can be risks of people who violate the rules…in other words …cheat.

We had that experience. A son of an officer of the company got on-line and violated the rules. He was caught "in the act" and lost his privilege to use the computer on-line. He was caught by me because I was monitoring the computer activity from a terminal at home. I had agreed to do this monitoring from home when management approved the outside access. We had a lot of security on the computer to protect critical or classified data.

The computer club members had accounts for training purposes. The club members were permitted to use the computer outside of business hours when the computer was not being used for the business of the company. The club accounts had restricted access and limited functionality. The kid who violated the rules had acquired the password of an employee. Instead of using the Computer club restricted account he was using an employee's business account.

Since I was the one to "blow the whistle" on a VP's son, it put me in a very uncomfortable position....for the remainder of my career.

Hazeljean Cheeseman Adams
HACKER PATROL

I DON'T CARE WHO YOU DADDY IS!

HOME COMPUTERS

Also in the early 1980's home computers became available. Several employees purchased computers for their homes. As an alternative to carrying home terminals to use on-line to the company computer, an employee could attach a modem to the telephone and use their home computer as a terminal.

Modems were expensive at the time. So the computer club initiated a project to build modems for the members.

The part of the modem that was used to attach the phone was called an acoustic coupler. The computer club learned of a company in our area that manufactured these couplers.

Also this company discarded any couplers that had a slight defect.

So the computer club members, including my nephew and me, made trips to the company's dump-site to retrieve the discarded couplers. Yes I was the ONLY Woman and ONLY Manager that was involved in this activity. We then built acoustic couplers for the club members to use from their homes.

"GET HER OUT OF MY OFFICE"

During this period personal computers were becoming the primary computing tool in the workplace. The era of the mainframe computer was fading away. But many of the older managers in the company were not convinced.

One of the senior engineering managers was not convinced that "his" engineers needed computers or terminals on their desks. I did not report directly to him at this time, but he had to approve budgets for computer equipment for the engineering organization. Of course I had worked with him and for him prior to this time and knew him well. I had many disagreements with him over the years.

He yelled at me and treated me like "one of the guys", which is what I wanted.

After I became the manager of Engineering Computer Facilities it was my responsibility to keep the engineering community with "state of the art" tools.

I was constantly "fighting" with the engineering managers to approve budgets to acquire personal computers. One day I was in a manager's office trying to convince him to approve one of these budgets. When he was loosing the argument he yelled to his secretary, "Get her out of my office". My comment to him was "well you are really getting desperate when you need to get your secretary to help you".

In spite of being a female and my high risk adventures, I was able to survive in this management position for several years. The computer organization experienced significant growth during this period. It was an exciting time for me. And in spite of all of the subsequent battles over budgets, I

"The Only Woman"

saw my dream of "A terminal or computer on every desk" come true.

RADIO INTERVIEW
"A STORM IN A TEAPOT"

In addition to teaching for my company, I did training as a volunteer in local organizations. I taught a microprocessing class at a local conference sponsored by IEEE. (I was the ONLY Woman in the local IEEE group also). I also often went to local schools to talk about careers in the computer field. I also participated in training programs for Junior Achievement and Girl Scouts.

As a result of some of my community activities, I was asked to be interviewed by a local radio station. I agreed and it was a harmless interview. It was about my career in general and some of the community projects. I am sure the

"The Only Woman"

interview included questions regarding my "non traditional" role for woman. I said nothing about my employer except stating where I worked.

Wow. did I get in trouble!!! I am sure guys did this all the time. But the Public Relations Director at my place of employment was enraged that I had not received prior approval for the interview. The company did have a policy that employees had to get approval for press releases involving company business. But I did not consider this company business.

Well, my boss defended my position. But I was still "in hot water". Fortunately, a friend had taped the interview. So I provided the tape which proved that I had said nothing negative about the company. Did they think I was really that naïve? I guess they were just paranoid that I would say something negative regarding treatment of woman by the organization. In later years I was able to see my employee folder. This incident remained on my record as a negative mark.

FIRST WOMAN DIRECTOR
GLASS CEILING SLIGHTLY ELEVATED

In the mid-1980's my company was acquired by a New York City based company. As a result several computer departments in the company were merged resulting in lay-offs, buy-outs etc.

Fortunately I survived the merger and all the cuts. And about four years after the merger, I became the first and ONLY woman Director in the new company.

In the Director position I had significantly more responsibility. In the Manager position I was managing the computer and personnel that supported only engineering and technical application. In my new position I also became responsible for all the Management Information systems. I was responsible for managing the entire budget of all the company's computer hardware, software, and support personnel. This was a giant step from my previous position.

Also in my new position I no longer had time to stay up-to-date technically. But I did stay up-to-date technically on my own time. And with ten to twelve hour workdays, my "own" time was shrinking.

Hazeljean Cheeseman Adams
MANAGER'S RETREAT

"YOU HAVE THE PICK OF THE CROP

BUT WHAT A CROP FAILURE"

CONFERENCES

At many conferences and retreats, I was the ONLY woman. The female waitresses were always so shocked to see me there. Many of the waitresses treated me like a "hero". I was always given special treatment by them. I remember at one retreat I was the ONLY woman at a large banquet table. A waitress said to me "You are so lucky to be the ONLY WOMAN with all these men." My response was "Yes quantity, but not quality". She looked around the room and said: "You are right"

At most conferences we all know that people play "hooky" and don't attend all sessions. If there are one hundred men at the conference no one would notice if one of them was missing. However if I missed a meeting it was obvious. As a result I could not play hooky and go golfing or partying.

At many meetings the speakers addressed the group saying "Gentlemen" not even noticing that I was there. Others would addressed the group as "Gentlemen and lady" or "Gentlemen and my name"

At one conference Joe Theisman, the quarterback, was the speaker. When he entered the room, I was chatting with my boss. I guess I had a shocked look on my face. My boss made some comment like why that expression. I said "what a contrast with the rest of the guys in this room". Most were short, bald, and had stock options. Theisman was tall, well built, tanned, and handsome. The comparison was striking.

HOW I SURVIVED AGAINST MANY ODDS
VARIETY WAS MY MOTTO

During my career I had many different jobs in a variety of areas. I was fortunate to have the opportunities, but on the other hand I often agreed to do jobs that others did not want. No matter how bad the assignment I was always willing to try.

I did programming, wrote manuals, wrote proposals, taught programming to company personnel as well as customers, and managed a variety of projects. And I was always the ONLY WOMAN until recent years.

Hazeljean Cheeseman Adams

In my early career I taught FORTRAN programming to Engineers. Most of the older engineers had no formal computer training in college. The students were all men.

When I returned to company I traveled and taught programming at government facilities and military bases... again my students were all men. When I taught at a military base I was usually the ONLY woman in the whole hotel.

SPECIAL PROJECTS

I was often on "loan" to other departments and projects where they needed computer expertise but not require a permanent computer staff. I worked for several years on a highly classified project. It took several months to get a clearance. Anyone without a clearance was not permitted to be unescorted in the building. As a result, I had to be escorted (by a male) to the rest room until I received a clearance. Aside: he did stay outside the door.

As a programmer/analyst I had many interesting assignments. Since I moved around in the company I worked in many diverse application areas. I was involved in software development for satellite tracking systems; lighter than air vehicle applications; tire test equipment processors; Space thermo programs; AWACS surveillance; CAD CAM IC design; operation research applications; flight simulators; surveillance and tracking system; uranium enrichment; parallel processor operating system software; microprocessor operating systems; real time data acquisition and control; manufacturing monitoring and scheduling systems; business management systems; and Personal Computer applications …which I continue to do in my "retirement".

I programmed in many programming languages during my career. In the computer field it has always been necessary to continue learning as the technology changed.

In the early years I programmed in machine and assembler languages for several different computers. When higher level languages were developed I programmed in: FORTRAN. COBOL, ALGOL, PL1, BASIC, VISUAL BASIC, and C++.

"The Only Woman"

The latter two languages were for Personal Computer Applications.

HARASSMENT

During my career I experienced sexual harassment many times. However only in one incident, the harasser was my supervisor. I felt it really was only sexual harassment if the harasser had the power to jeopardize my career. The one legitimate case happened when I was on a trip with the supervisor. At that time suing was not an option. Also it was a situation of his word against mine. Guess who would be believed.

The way I handled was to pick up the phone to call his wife. It worked. But I despise this guy to this day. Fortunately he did not have an opportunity to affect my career, because I was only with the company for a short

"The Only Woman"

time after that. But this incident did influence my decision to leave the company.

As a manager I experienced true sexual harassment by managers towards other woman in the organization. They usually pick on vulnerable woman who did not have a lot of options in there lives. Also until recent laws were passed most of the women had no choice but to leave the company to avoid the problem. These men were always protected by their "old boy's network".

Several male managers had harassed woman for years. The whole company knew about it. It became a joke in the company and outside the company. Nothing was ever done about it. They were always protected by their superiors (males of course).

When the company was acquired and new management came in, a female employee finally blew the whistle on one of the longtime offenders. I am sure she thought the new acquiring company's officials would do something about it.

The situation was properly handled by the new management. If the perpetrator had been reported to the previous management, it would have been buried by the "old boy's" network. But I do not know if that occurred. There may not have been reports by the woman earlier because of fear.

The other side…possible false accusation of harassment I also had male managers who I believe were falsely accused of harassment. My opinion is they were reported because the accusing employees had received negative evaluations.

But since there were no witnesses to these events, I cannot say for sure. These situations were resolved by having the females report to a different manager. This made my job more difficult because reporting to a different manager was not a logical situation for the functions they performed. This made management of the employees and the work performed very awkward.

DEALING WITH THE UNION

Since I was always responsible for installing computer equipment and providing computers supplies, I had many issues with the union. I am a strong believer in doing things in a logical "least-cost" way for the benefit of the company.

Also it was my responsibility to keep the company's computers running 24/7. This required that equipment be installed in a timely fashion and supplies available when needed. The union had their rules, which I felt were antiquated regarding the new technologies.

An example: When we started installing Personal Computers on engineer's desks, the union insisted it was their function to unpack the Personal Computers. This was totally impractical. They did not have the expertise to install the Personal Computers. Unpacking the computer took about 5 minutes, while the total set-up and installation of software, network etc. could take several hours. It was impractical to wait for a union person to come to unpack each computer. I finally had the union representative come to my office and I showed him what was involved in unpacking a Personal Computer, as he watched me unpack my own. I won this one, but lost many of these battles with the union and had many grievances over the years. Being involved in this technology growth era I was always fighting the status-quo.

PRESSURE FROM VP
TO PROCURE COMPUTERS FROM "HIS" PREFERRED COMPANY

Since we were a Defense Department Supplier, we had very specific rules regarding procurement procedures. There was a selection committee that evaluated all proposals. I was on the committee to evaluate the proposals from the technical view point. i.e. Which product best satisfied the technical requirement.

Actually two guys who worked for me did the detailed review. They then presented it to me and we jointly selected the best product technically. This included not only the computer hardware but maintenance and support of the product on an on-going basis. Two companies might have equivalent hardware, but different support proposals. In that case the support proposal became the deciding factor.

We received proposals with no company names, so that there was no possibility to select on some personal bias. A procurement person was on the committee to review the cost proposal. The technical people never knew the cost proposal until after the technical decision was made. We followed all the rules…this WAS company policy. It was more than company policy, it was mandatory when doing business for the Defense Department.

A VP in the company had some type of connection with one of the proposing companies. I was never quite sure what the real connection was. I felt that he had ownership in the company which would have been blatantly illegal. There was a large procurement pending for personal computers. This VP came to my office several times to try to pressure me to sway the decision.

"The Only Woman"

And I said NO WAY in every way I knew how. The pressure was so intense that I became physically sick. I came close to calling a lawyer for the first time in my career. I finally went to my boss and asked to be removed from the selection committee. The two guys who worked for me took my place. Also the last time this officer came to my office he knew all the cost estimates, which should not have been available to him. So apparently he was putting the squeeze on someone else, and it worked.

Of course at the time I thought he was trying his pressure on me because I was a female and might cave in. Fortunately the timing was in my favor because the new division management knew this guy's modus operendi and believed my story. I heard later this VP tried to get me fired. If he had, there would have been a suit. I had lots of witnesses and I documented every conversation that I had with him. Also shortly after this he was caught with other improprieties and was suspended. But he was suspended with full pay. Real punishment?

Subsequently, I heard that this VP had done similar "illegal" things for several years in the company and it was apparently covered up. So he obviously had a "friend" higher up protecting him. I put illegal in quotes because, in my various discussions with this guy, I am sure he had a definition of integrity and legality that was very different from mine.

BOSS'S NIGHT

The local secretary's organization had a banquet once a year called boss's night. All the secretaries hosted their boss. The speaker was a football coach at the local university. He had previously been relieved of his position as the coach at a large prominent university. He was quite well-know across the country.

As a part of his speech he started to tell a joke. He stopped in mid-stream and explained that since this was a joke about sports, the woman wound probably not understands. Well I was the only woman manager in the room and of course being an avid sports fan was very insulted by this outward chauvinist comment by a man of his stature. (Note this was the late 1980's). I was tempted to walk out but did not want to embarrass my secretary. But the response from the secretaries was overwhelming and made up for me not walking out. He was loudly booed by all of the women in the room.

This is not the end of the story. I am an avid football fan and my husband and I had season tickets for the local college football games. In fact, my husband was a professor at this university and was on the athletic committee at the time. When I went home and told him about the coach putting his foot in his mouth, my husband was shocked.

Well during that season we attended all the games even though I booed the coach at every opportunity. At one game he called a pass for the last play of the game with 2 yards to go. As a result, we lost the game. I told my husband that I was going to the gate where the coach passes through and give the coach my opinion of his last play call. And my husband said "oh no" or something to that effect. Of course I said "watch me". Well what I said to the coach is not for

"The Only Woman"

publication. But I was not alone…there were several guys also yelling at him.

I had threatened to discontinue buying season tickets. But this coach was a total flop and did not last long at the university.

DOUBLE STANDARD ISSUE: FRIENDS WITH SUBORDINATES

As a Director and Manager, I could not be friends with woman (or men for that matter) that worked for me. This was definitely a double standard. The male managers drank, golfed, and were friends with guys that worked for them. That was accepted. Some even had affairs with the woman that worked for them. And this conduct did not alter there career path. Many of those guys are still in high positions in the company.

But several times in my career I was accused of showing a preference towards women who were my friends. By the way these women were my friends long before I became a

"The Only Woman"

manager. As a result I could not associate with woman that worked for me without feeling uncomfortable. None of these accusations were valid, but they damaged my reputation as well as caused harm to the other woman involved. The implication was that a female could not make a fair logical decision as a manager. In addition to altering careers, this is an unfair influence on one's personal life.

We all know that the "good old boys" network is the reason that most of the male mangers acquired their positions. Many were not qualified for the position but received the position because of a friend higher up in the organization.

Later in my career I should have been a mentor to the younger woman, but it was not permitted to do so, without false accusation of patronizing.

DOUBLE STANDARD: EMOTIONS

Emotion is another area where double standards still exist. If a woman gets mad and shows emotions in a management situation, she is called an "emotional woman" or she has PMS or going through menopause.

But the male managers have knock down drag out fights, and that is OK??? "Boys will be boys" I guess.

I was always very careful during my whole career to control my emotions. As I stated earlier no matter how mad I got, I walked away. Then at a later time and with a cooler head I responded.

"The Only Woman"

If anyone, male or female, started a "public" argument with me I walked away. I always felt that in a public argument it is unclear to the witnesses which person is the fool.

"RETIREMENT"

I was offered and took an early retirement incentive plan….again the ONLY woman. This was offered to 25 Managers and Directors. I immediately took a part time teaching position at a local university. I taught mathematics and computer science courses.

In this environment I was finally not the ONLY woman. By teaching I was able to keep up-to-date with the constantly changing computer technology.

The first summer break of teaching, I became bored. And decided to volunteer to work for John Kenley and the Kenley Players. They were putting on musicals in my area. I began as a volunteer and became a part-time employee. Since I had a computer background, I trained the tickets sales people to use the computerized ticket system.

In the middle of the summer Mr. Kenley lost his accountant. He asked me to continue and do the accounting for the company. This was a definite divergence from my long career in the engineering and technical field. Of course I had accounting courses in college and also had managed budgets for the years that I was a manger and director. I enjoyed this experience and of course was not the only woman.

I continue to work as a volunteer to support Web sites for local non-profit organizations. Also I do one-on-one training and computer support for church friends and others in the community. I continue to do consulting and software development in my "spare" time.

SUMMARY

In summary, I had an interesting and challenging career and really have no regrets. However being the ONLY woman made my life different, but different is not necessarily a negative thing. There were a lot of negative and frustrating times. There were also some good guys that supported me and helped me along the way. Not many…but thank goodness for the few.

Made in the USA
Monee, IL
24 January 2023